INITIAL CONDITIONS

INITIAL CONDITIONS

Julie Benesh

Saddle Road Press

Saddle Road Press
Ithaca, New York
saddleroadpress.com

Book design and cover image by Don Mitchell
Author photo by: Alan Luntz

ISBN 9798987954140
Library of Congress Control Number: 2023945919

Books by Julie Benesh
About Time

CONTENTS

I

II

III

I

ON THE CONSTANCY OF FORGETTING

Every time we remember some forgotten moment in a way that illuminates the present or causes the present to mediate some past, then the boundaries we thought were there between past, present and future dissolve, if only for the time that is the poem.
—Tess Gallagher, The Poem as Time Machine, 1979

THE INFINITE COMINGS OF AGE

At the open   graveside of your then-husband's
grandfather, yourself long out of grandparents
by then, your mother buried five years, you lift your hand,
dreamily releasing the fragrance: rosemary and clove
serum from your hair, and the first time,
that thing you thought could never happen to you, you
were always so cautious and fearful, you are stung in the finger
by a bee, and before you can say *anaphylaxis*
you remember that burly bookstore jock you were made to fire
a decade before, when things were different, but not all that
different,
and how bee sting reactions get worse every time, *sensitization*,
though you'd think they should get less bad, *desensitization*,
and you are not that different, either, just different
enough to know how to *deploy employees to more appropriate
opportunities*,
as if it were a favor, and honeybees die after just one sting,
but your ex-husband will live on, more or less, as will you.

TRAJECTORY

On our first date, I left nothing to chance,
wearing (advised by my male friends) my black
sweater with the bright stripes across the bust.
      We both had Beef Wellington and I spit
the paté discreetly into my hand,
mortified, while "Melt with You" was playing,
as you gazed at me, like I was night sky,
a star interviewed on the red carpet.
      Later I'd learn that Lindemann's theory
says melting occurs when the amplitude
of atomic vibration, equalized,
creates harmony, common frequency,
and reasonable agreement;
    thus, while burning, alone, we would,
together, melt.

WAKE UP

with a hodgepodge pile of stuff
to make a bouillabaisse or salad of leaves

build a mansion or lean-to shack
protect from elements and enemies

fashion a tiara or a sassy sash
so as not to scare the children

      [and by the way, this test is timed
      and no one knows its individually specific duration
      between 0 and 48,000 wakes]

who wake up with some of your stuff
and some stuff left by someone
who saw yours or wore their shiny tiara
in a coffee shop or database
reflecting righteous shelter/land/crops

to keep it all going   to leave
something better
in your wake

AFTER NEMEROV

St. Howard would float down Lindell,
sink on Skinker, inches above the ground;
beaming dreamy, feeling groovy, like a mirror
blessing our youthful union. We called
him Uncle: it was all about us.

Write what you know. That should leave
you with a lot of free time.

We knew nothing but the warm give
of our bodies; their sweet, swelling
scent. I tried to write poems
not knowing

A lot happens by accident in poetry

that journal they made fun
of, the one that took everyone
would not take me, so cursed
was I by joy.

I have a plot, but not much happens.

We didn't know
those years were but
a short break
from heartbreak,
not its end.

I sometimes talk about the making
of a poem within the poem:

A bird's nest of dreams, detritus fused
with snot, tears; all that assorted effluvia.
It's not much, is it? But

I love all my children even the squat,
ugly ones

sacred enough for me now, the knowing, broken
Auntie beaming blessings of her own.

Plus Ça Change

That swagger-daddy on the Red Line
     el asks the auntie
if she's Spanish   poor lady
he requests a sex act   she's Italian
she won't muster outrage   giggles, shakes her head
and we roll our eyes   on their joint behalf
     cuz, pro-forma
they both know   bois will be bois
it don't hurt to try   from his perspective

nature has rhythms   bodies breathe
digest and reproduce   seasons into
predictable   unpredictable inevitability

     forest fires
smolder over   gender revelations
making space   new landscapes
replicating infinite   variations.

  we are on the same train
they sat here   we'll sit there
wondering how   chill as ever
     this world
could die   having so far
since world began   only rendered life
     immortal.

REMEMBERING THE SABBATH

When I get those Sunday scaries, those Sunday
scaries spreading dread like carbon monoxide,
low barometric pressure of the soul, and I want,

when I get those Sunday scaries, to avoid
a thousand dollars' worth of coral activewear,
consuming an entire French silk pie,

plucking bald brows, texting exes, hacking
hipster bangs, innovating new martini recipes,
to avoid Sunday scaries, I land on Google

Street View, seeking a glimmer, shimmer, trigger;
ghostly gasping greeting from the past places left
unattended: that strip mall I worked at during my divorce,

the condo where lightning struck like a bomb,
that gym where I worked off the frozen custard
from that shop with the peaked roof: imagining

current constituents suffering, suppressing Sunday
scaries: recreating, procreating, populating, tearing down,
clearing out, shoring up, like bellows reanimating, picking

up where I left off, until one scary Sunday in the future,
I will Google my current abandoned past present here,

in anticipation of anticipating
the anticipation of nostalgia,
remembering the Sabbath.
keeping it holy.

CARAPACE

In the almost spring
as the white sky
tries to rain

Lana is afraid
of that empty Shell station
by the old highway exit,
like the cemetery at the end
of our block   its spirits,
yet fears no living exoskeleton,
ushering pests to safe new homes:
compassionate cockroach concierge,

whereas I murder by proxy with shrink-
wrapped, pre-shelled lobster meat
to throw on a charcoal grill
and consume in an act
of transubstantiation.

She does not yet know that Earth
is a graveyard.

It's all recycling, for better or worse:
the wages of life are shells;
the first currency, shells
hide, protect, outlast
their host. Fossils
make the world
go around; fossils
fossils, the whole
way down.

That electric car billionaire plans
to abandon this space station:
Are we running out or moving on?

Lana believes in reincarnation; together
we ponder the immortal past: ghosts
of men in uniform, names squiggle-stitched
above their pockets, wiping windshields clean.

THOSE WHO DON'T BELIEVE IN GHOSTS

may or may not own a television
or allow children to eat ice cream;
might worship at the big white church
or the dark cathedral, or the altar
of consumer goods or dynastic fortunes.

must live in the present
as the slimmest of gifts,
mere stocking-stuffers;
or the future: master
the universe, smart
in-every-room,
die with all the jacks.

Deniers of empathies
or downright enemies

in your fancy-crap cars
off to crap-fancy jobs
avoiding eye contact

with pedestrians who try
to cross the street in the rain
splashed by rushed puddles
of your imminent redundancy.

Praise yourselves,
faking your making!

The lucky blessed:
among the haunt
or be haunted,
you, the haunters.

Mausoleums teem with your ilk,
despite the logical impossibility,
the irony of your existence.

Those who

don't see   the ghosts
doomed to be   the ghosts.

SPARE

Spare me the organ recital
such music only decomposes
I want to know how not to be
ashamed of my panniculus
my varicosities and lipid count
how not to trigger a spiral
      into worseness unto aboulia

Spare me your liturgy of forgetfulness
subtle arguments you draw
      that end in draws
your litany of filtered memories
like a junk drawer of dreams
you mistake for ours

Spare me your
semiotics of piety
to be a martyr is grave
    as victim is gravity
    as default

tell me how you talk yourself up
in the morning
down at night to sleep

under the same dark blanket
as the rest of us
the none of us who ever
were or ever will
be spared

Corpse Pose

At the end of the day, on my way to yoga, the sun is yet to set,
and no crepuscular rats dart through snowbanks like they did the
night before, so far as I can see; the days are getting longer.
First to the studio, I take my favorite spot, at the end, where I
never used to want to be; hot yoga which I never used to think
I'd like, but I love the routine of it unspooling as always: child's
pose, sun salutations, lunges, warrior sequence, forward fold, tree,
pyramid, goddess, locust, crunches, bridge, pigeon, happy baby,
twists, legs up the wall. I sip my water and lie down for *savasana*
imagining the sweet, spicy chai I will brew when I get home, and
an essay I wrote this morning and I wonder whether the word
"deficit" was a word I shouldn't have used, in that essay, and I
am only supposed to think about "now," and my breath and my
easeful body, not Past Essay and Future Chai, and it occurs to
me, deficit can be another word for asset, just as surfeit can be
too much extra, like a deficit of rats in the snowbanks is for me,
better than a surfeit; and "now" can be longer, much longer, than
the time it takes to walk two blocks through the snowy streets and
brew a cup of chai, long as a late winter's evening, long as a life.

Before We Met

From a decade away I could hear
the shimmer of heat from your barbecue.

I am sure you wish you knew me then.
I was that peckish princess: eyes

like plastic plates from Target;
dudes on the el   snapping/swapping/selling
pix of my sweet-sandaled feet.

That train
roiling me to sleep;
lulling me awake.

My hair whiffed cilantro and ginger marinade;
would not stop growing under my crown;
convinced me I'd get what I wanted,
so saucy was I on the outside.

WAVICLE

Manometers measure pressure
but the act of observation
changes the observed. Bitter pattern
is like spewing iron dust on paper
over magnet, and a ghost traces remnants
of radiation that strayed.

Keepers preserve magnetism and latent
heat overcomes attractive forces.
Neutral equilibrium suggests stability but, *moi*...
I am not, by definition, a hot heat keeper, as vectors
measure distance, not displacement, i.e.,

we live together but are, indisputably,
alone and a wavicle is just a cute nickname for a photon:
wave plus particle, a tabloid's
celebrity couple's portmanteau.

Overtone is, likewise, strictly musical,
So, perversion is not of unusual significance
and horizontal intensity is stable only in Britain,
fluctuating everywhere else, which makes no sense.

Cascade processes occur in stages (like cancer
in us animals, or irreconcilability in these makeshift
social pods we humans call marriage)

and damped...oscillation...
slows...itself...down, whereas
entropy accelerates dis or der
grad u al ly,
Sl ud e n d   y

SINCE YOU'VE BEEN GONE

I rode that proverbial horse
to some more proverbial rodeos.
Back in the saddle.

I took those pills you wanted
me to. You got that operation.
Isn't it ironic? Which is not to say

coincidental, not at all. Quite the opposite.
Which is in itself ironic, so, same difference.
You thought I would starve or, at best,

find a sugar daddy to feed me ribeye
and frozen custard. But as I said at the time,
that's too easy. You know me: gotta do it my own way.

Since you've been gone I've mostly been begged
to stay—a few exceptions make the rule
credible; remind me of the standard

I set, the margin. Science is replicable; math
logical. That never changes. But humans
are of science without having to know science

much at all. I recall your hate for random weirdness
and your blindness to your own, the only kind
that really matters. You know what they say

about hindsight, how it twists every cliche,
like, well, you know what

WALK

Your eyes meet over the rat corpse
in rueful, mute acknowledgment
What you gonna do?—it's the city…

sidewalks framed in wrought iron, geraniums
in planters, squirrels raiding bird feeders,
crystal spider web gleams from a branch

swaying overhead. Everybody's
gotta eat, breathe and reproduce,
or at least produce.

That wrapper you drop in the bin
will become bird's nest for a crow
that will become a snack for the dog

whose owner meets your eye
over the rat corpse, pulls on the leash
and walks away

as you walk on alone, the bottom-heavy
common denominator of your
every experience.

THE SPRING-BRINGER

breaks dawn a little earlier every day,
waking you like a sweet puppy
you train without even trying.
Cues robins. One morning you smell his breath,
botanical, and its nuance caresses
you like a shower, thunder and all.
Who's training whom? He's the cruelest flirt in the wasted land:
literally blowing hot and cold; your stagnant bits thaw, terrible/
slow/lovely
(just like Mrs. Parker said). That thing, those things,
all the things you gave up without even meaning
to and then like riding a bike you ride
them all, you pick up all the abandoned brushes, paint (wall) and
paint (canvas), and hair and toilet, and even if—*hell,*
especially if—you don't believe that Jesus
is risen, something has risen in your own doughy limbs. Praise
that breadcrumbing, immature, inevitable spring-bringer
for the dampening air, the softening earth, the buds; the crocuses
you bend to stroke to life; colors green, and green, and green
and pink and yellow and violet; that old May song
ringing from every tower.

After Thomas Lux "The Joybringer"

Aubade

The future's a whale that doesn't target
us, particularly: drinks its ocean,
filters needed nutrients, expels the rest.

The biggest-eyed kitten's a trained assassin,
but even she can learn to mother a bird.
We never blame the faster prey

for starving the predator,
and confuse the light of dawn
with the end of days.

What comes for us is
                            nothing
compared to what we do,
                                    ourselves
to   ourselves,
pulling

              every

                    trigger

Karma, by Another Name

Babe?! Did you hear the clatter in the kitchen? The dog has gobbled down our dinner…again!

When we come back, from, you, know, *beyond,* one of us is gonna be him. We probably already were! We probably take turns as dog, me, you; you, me, dog; you, dog, me. Checks, balances; mutually assured preservation, life after life.

Comforting thought…so…pizza or Chinese?

When in doubt, do both. Chianti, jasmine tea, potstickers…

…egg rolls, sausage and cheese, cannoli and fortune cookies.

Remember that place we used to go to finish each others'…

…meals?   …sentences!

Fornetto Mei. The pizza with the red grapes…We sat by the oven on cold winter nights, talking about Nietzsche, watching the cook with the little long-handled…shovel…

paddle…?   *Peel!*

The husband was Italian, the wife Chinese; the food: not fusion, more…

…eclectic   complementary.

Well, but not free.

With an *e*…Remember in Paris? The bakery lady yelling *"pas compris"* when you snagged that macaroon…

Yin and yang? Like us?

...that sweet hot chili oil went with everything, made it all...

...better, right?   ...*elevated.*

Like you!

Look who's complimentary. With an *I!*

When You Spot Your Flower

shooting sunward, every word:
redacted, rejected; yields a dozen pages
more. There are so many ways to mother:

watching ice melt to water, water gather
itself to steam, reason yield to mystery,
crassness to mastery, over and over,
predictable as dawn.

You want to be a baby again; you want
to be new?

Nurse your yearning and starve ambition.
I double dare you.

I swear, clever friend, sometimes I wish
I had a thousand lives; and when I find
my orchid, whose very roots need light,
I'm going to ask her to dance, gamble
for gambol, because, in the end,
where it matters, what's the difference
between laughter and prayer?

STANDARD TIME

Think of it as mood lighting. Even alpha Apollo
needs a rest. Even if you merry Christmas
with the best of them, strip a Christian and out pops
a naked pagan, pious in their own way, loins warming
by the fire. We are not equatorial, so follow

me as spring follows winter, slow yet relentless,
inevitable as death. The best holidays are clustered
where we need them, around the darkest times
of year when ritual promises renewal. *Cuffing
season*, the kids call it.

Fanning out to frame them, the glowing wreath
of minor constellations: Gothic Halloween,
shadowy Groundhog Day, and commercial cousin:
red-teddied Valentine, shaking (martyred)
moneymaker; fractals equidistant between solstice
and equinox.

You say: summer bodies are forged in winter.
I say: we need energy to hibernate. Have more stuffing
and another piece of pie; let that blood drain brain to gut.
In six months time, that Great Lake—arctic,
berged with ice—will keep us cool,
while the rest of the city swelters.

LOOP

Between the afternoon and dusk outside
the subway stop at State and Grand talking
about plumbing fixtures, ostensibly,

when something someone said some way or heard
reminded of that one time in Paris,
arguing, I'd said, outside the Metro

look at the moon and we'd looked at the moon
like a swelling belly replete with both
presence and prescience and you proclaimed

that moment taught you so much about   your
capacity for wonder and delight
and I spat out my coffee and we still

go on going on like trains underground
or vessels/tunnels/tracks holding them safe.

BIRDS OF THE MIDWEST

The July I was fifteen, weekdays, after my dad
left for work, Mom and I would don bright blouses
to go visit his father,
my only remaining grandparent,
at St. Luke's Hospital,
about a two mile, ten-minute drive.

On the way we might stop for a dollar's worth of gas,
and Shorty would pump it, waving his lit cigarette
as he jabbered, I bracing for an explosion as my mom
nodded and murmured in a way he clearly interpreted
as encouraging. Once I sighed, audibly, and he ducked
his head saying, "Well, I'll let you go." My mother
scolded me as we pulled away and quit
taking me there, but I figured I did her a solid,
quite possibly saving both our lives.

The nurses annoyed me by referring to my grandpa
as my mother's father. *In-law,* I would add under my breath.
In-law, they would repeat, condescendingly, pursing lips
and rolling eyes. But someone had to stick up for her, give her credit.

After the visit, before I would take off to flirt and gossip
at the public pool, we usually had lunch at the coffee shop
across the street from the hospital.

One day I became distraught that the fried chicken
I had ordered tasted both familiar and yet wrong
and I imagined it was turkey, what I thought turkey
would taste like fried, so tough, dry and flavorless
I couldn't finish it. "Well, just don't order
it again," said my mom, polite as ever.

One rainy Saturday, my parents went together
to the hospital. and must have let in the robin
I watched career off the walls of our tiny house.
Our three cats watched too, and it saw them.

I knew there was a way to take a towel and shoo
it out, but I was outnumbered. Overwhelmed,
I retreated, defeated into my walk-in closet of a bedroom,
closed the door and nestled to sleep immediately,
waking a couple hours later when my parents
returned. I emerged, cotton-mouthed and groggy,
shaking my head, asking, *Where's the bird?* What bird?
A robin got in... Are you sure you didn't dream it? *Yes—the cats went
crazy.* We found something on the floor
by the cats' dish that looked like a yellow beak.
But where were the feathers, the bones, the blood?

Grandpa survived and went home to his mansion.
A few years later, when I was in college, my parents
sold our house to move in to care for him. Thanksgiving break
we walked through our empty nest,
footfalls echoing, and I started to cry.
Did you ever find more remains of that bird? Never.

Another Thanksgiving, my mother ten years gone, a friend
deep-fried a turkey. Like gas pump-adjacent arm-waving, smoke
breaks, a dangerous undertaking; had to be done outside;
could it possibly be worth it? It sounded gross. I braced.
Its taste exploded like nothing imagined, so juicy
and delicious I wanted to consume leave no trace, make my red
blood and wishbone, my flightless feathers become so light
and unassuming as to rise and rise and rise, invisible.

ON THE WAY TO CONCEPTION

My parents loved each other but it's unlikely no one was harmed
or sold on the long, broad path to my conception,
and as for fidelity, my mitochondrial DNA is Brit
all the way to the damsel du chambre of Queen Philippa,
born in Tonbridge Castle, mother unknown, fathered
by Edward's ambidextrous favorite.

Some of my auxiliary genes marched with Strongbow,
in their sturdy separate packaging, then, centuries
hence, met again, more intimate, in colonial America,
then the Midwest, Irish mingling with Czechs and Swedes.

Lest that sound like incest jest, let's confess:
we are all related in multiple ways, not just to each other
but the whole animal kingdom, to plants, to the expanding stars.

And it's reductive to think fate and identity
is all DNA; some genes we turn
on and off with our behavior / actions / habits
and more than nature is nurture, still transmissible,

as even when not discussed aloud, we get a sense
of what happened before, inside the family walls
from what is unsaid; broken chains remember
each other in the dark, like healed vasectomies.

And there are so many kinds of cultural pedigrees,
histories, taxonomies, traditions, besides the family
tree: the org chart, the resume, the chain of mentoring,
and studies that build on studies and beget new studies,
books that talk to books of yore, and poems to poems past.

Some, like tiny lost civilizations, fall out of fashion's favor,
disappear, to be dragged back later by archaeological inclination,

so it doesn't matter that I never had children
(or if your children or theirs don't have children),
because we all leave our willful traces: kaleidoscopes
continually fluctuating; indestructible fractals of the universe.

The Words

If only I could iterate my life
like a poem or a piece of prose

I could experience infinite possibility,
and progress through regression.

I'd evolve through devolution;
time's arrow would have nothing on me.

Like the past, to change one word of text
changes totality. But this revision is real:

one hand replaces and erases
all that came before. The other

alone enables what the future deems inevitable.
To live in the body is to live in seeds: egg,

chicken; acorn, oak. Fate is what's left over when all else
is redacted: what stays is what reprises. It's possible

to be a plot device, a minor character, in someone else's drama:
a footnote; marginalia, a garnish which could turn postmodern
                              entrée, centered

and amplified. You say today is a chimera,
elusive as hummingbird;

I say it lasts forever, like a fish-feasted fisherman who becomes a
feast for fishes; his progeny and theirs finding eternal sustenance,
each one overlapping the other.
The physicists agree with Nietzsche

that everything happened in infinite variations
and will again forever. That mistake I made with my mother?

I can redeem (or compound) it with my lover.
In the end when they ask would I do it again

I'll shake my head: where does one draft
end and another begin?

After Adrienne Su, "The Days"

THE CONSTANCY OF FORGETTING

When I wake up and nothing hurts,
or something hurts in a soft way:
like a shin-twinge, radiating, muscular,
reminding me I can still break and come

back stronger, or even when a small
discomfort comforts: dry mouth, a rumble
of hunger or tingle of neuropathy, the civil
defense sirens silent, the sad trombones

and tiny violins mute as sleep, I remember
how I love when the weather forecast is wrong
in either direction, and how I thought physical therapy
was for the sedentary and then it cured my pain,

and while there may be no food in the fridge
there is food at the store my phone will pay
for with my job stress. I'm a good provider:
my silverfish are living their best lives,

feasting and weaving like wedding guests
in a painting by Breughel while the cats
pose decorative as Instagram billionairesses.
I have a panoply of invisible subscriptions

that no doubt keep the global economy
afloat. Also nothing's burning or even smells bad:
in my house or my fleshly abode: so much given
and chosen and dreamed and unimaginable,
the unlikelihood of any of us waking up

ever at all, let alone here and now together
in the careless flip of a blank new day
like no other and so many others: it's true
there are fates worse than clichés.

II

CONFESSION, WITH REDACTIONS

"Yet why not say what happened?"
— Robert Lowell, *Day by Day*

GIRLWOR(L)D

Been every version of that girl:
first as an urchin I'd, furtive, twirl a curl
of hair and poke it in my ear: weird and impure.

Nerd, curmudgeon, hermit, lurking jerk, working
on curbing, purging her absurdest quirks,
but forth they burst, making it worse.

I've learned (and learned and learned)
it's best to spurn
attention, lest I hurl,
inspiring your so-called mercy-murders,
or incur some other, similar, familiar, curses.
So though I'm verbal, if not verbose, no verses
(plural) I've unfurled have gone viral
or curried any favorable furor
let alone commercial fervor,
and I remain and ever return,
alert, in that awkward spiral
of words heard and unheard.

So I endure your urgent burdens
as that hurdling, hurling, hurt-ling girl:
ardent, learned, undeterred
by those burnished purgatories
of your making   waiting, deter-
mined, unable to hurry victory, for the   turn,
the future fertile, febrile curdle I need to   earn
to occur, first,
before the   burn
and   urn.

LOOKERS

"Your ma has eyes in the back of her head." She'd laugh and laugh as I looked and looked.

Before he was my father, he ate carrots to pass the eye test to go to war. He met my mother-to-be on a double date with her foul-mouthed cousin with whom she lived. Later he'd wait for her to get home from dates with other boys, sitting on her porch and chatting with her aunt and uncle. She was an orphan, skinny then, but with those killer breasts (which would eventually kill her). He was a catch, the son of a judge, track champ, movie star handsome.

I hovered behind them; nascent, watching, rooting: desperate to inherit his looks, her insight; desire strong enough to get me born: a random mixed breed, compromised, derivative, half-blind.

She saw me: then, later, always, dragging my fingers across the back of her scalp, under her hair, imagining I could almost see them, wondering how I could possibly keep overlooking anything so important.

THE COLOR OF MY EYES

Freezing today, and I'm a little numb
Looking out the window at billows of steam
That keep my body warm, but not so much the rest.

I have a to-do list but it's not written down
and I'm not the type to write things down
for the mere satisfaction of crossing them off.
I'd rather make a not-do list, but hoo-boy,
that'd take a while.

Some say winter is not, contrary to popular belief
the season of repose; that under the snow
is a gathering, even an orgy.

I see portents everywhere these days:
that CLOSE TOMORROW sign on the bank
promising a more intimate future or at least
a gesture toward solvency.

My dreams combine times and places,
even people, of my past like a film
poorly adapted from a dog-eared novel,

leading me to believe what I thought was a window
might be a painting, or, more likely, a foggy mirror.

I mean to say I'm a part of nature,
so nothing if not eternally hopeful.

After Tony Hoagland, "The Color of the Sky"

LINN JUNCTION

My father built the cabin by the river
himself, and built me a treehouse
on the riverbank and two kinds of swings:
one with a tire you sit on and one to hang
on upright. We found a wounded duckling
near the pond, and nursed it back to health.
I scraped my sternum raw on the Styrofoam
boogie board, shot arrows,
and played a game with darts
now outlawed; relieved myself in a bucket
or an outhouse.

It was not a good place for menses,
with no running water, due to a burst pipe
never fixed, but the meals outstanding, barbecue
on charcoal or wood my parents doused with gasoline
and threw a match at. We ate prime steaks
and my mother made cheese sauce on the electric stove
to top the baked potatoes, with salad and corn
from our garden up the hill.

We had a fishing boat we'd take out to camp
on sandbars, and my father would seine for minnows
and release armadas of crawdads.

He planted hundreds of trees by hand on that one acre,
and fed dozens of cats. The neighbor's dog used to carry
them around in his mouth, gently, a form of recreation
for each party.

My parents wanted to build their dream
home there and I don't remember
when I realized that railroad bridge
Dad put a hundred sparklers

on for 4th of July
the one with the walkway
added when that boy and girl
jumped to their death
to avoid the train,
would become a highway
over the river connecting
two sides of the city.

How To Be It

These are the first days of spring. The breeze at dawn
pumps petrichor to the tune of birds chirping relentless cheer;
that gap between pounding heart and sluggish mind. A woman
and cat lie in bed, waiting for the day to begin.

The cat says *let's eat breakfast then come back to bed,*
snuggle up together and go back to sleep again, full-bellied.
That is how cats process a change of seasons.

Woman and cat get up and head for the kitchen.
The cat wants a special treat this morning,
but considering the end of winter, the woman
can't help but think about her panniculus,
long swaddled like a beloved infant
too soon exposed and forced to learn to walk
and talk, as befitting spring.

The cat says *as long as we can jump and run, our bits*
are fine to swing as much as they need to for balance.
Let's get us up somewhere high and look on down
at everything like the queens we are. But the woma
is humbled by taxes due before she knows it, the torture
of details followed by the imagination of judgment
followed by the pain of payment: insult compounding injury.

The cat says *there's always catnip and laser pointers and Netflix.*
And the woman thinks about the three things she always thinks
about: clothes degrading into rags, indelible and undesirable
memories, errors of omission and commission. Outside,
day is brightening like an interrogation during a strip search.

The cat says *brunch is a civilized ritual that will put us right.*
But the woman looks at her bookcases: so many words,
so few of them hers. She remembers how, as a girl,

she set out to read the whole encyclopedia, believing
there was a secret message therein, meant for her alone.

The cat says *maybe we can just drink some water.*
So they drink some water which is, after all, one of the few
things they need, and of the many of which they are made.

After Stephen Dobyns, "How to Like It"

About Last Night

Setting: a workshop with some people
from work, my best friend from high school,
many strangers I was keen to impress, and Samuel Beckett.

He must have been a descendant of the Irish playwright,
although he was a compact Asian man and a philosophy
professor, both, coincidentally, like my waking life boyfriend,
and he had a cute poodle he kept needing to walk.

Peeled someone else's banana and ate too many cookies,
couldn't find the ladies' room and had to relieve
myself, discreetly, in the park next door where some bros
were playing basketball. Squatting, I worried about the hem
of my dress, and, worse, cameras documenting any exposure.

My best friend from high school was showing home movies
and, in several, my parents appeared, my father with long 1970s
sideburns and both with a lot of black still in their hair.

It seemed important that I say something about my libido:
fast, despite the Prozac, and strong, despite my age,
but I couldn't see how to work that in, how to explain
it was not on behalf of myself, I wished to speak, but the world.

TRIPPIN'

My parents never took me to Chicago claiming their VW bug
would only ever get as far from Cedar Rapids, Iowa as Winneconne,
Wisconsin, on Lake Winnebago, near Oshkosh where my dad's
Uncle lived, so the biggest city
I ever visited before 1975 was Madison.
(Now I know Chicago is closer, but they didn't want to go there.
My dad thought only losers lived in cities.)

We always left on a summer Saturday before dawn,
highway reflectors casting ghostly images.
I would lie on the hard gray backseat
breathing second hand cigarette smoke
listening to my parents murmur and rattle road maps.

One time the battery exploded right under my seat,
splattering my pinafore with acid.

So I'd never been to Chicago before the ninth grade field trip
that took four hours and cost forty dollars. My mother
was born in Chicago but moved to Iowa as a baby
and remembered nothing and was likely fearing for my life,
as when she thought Chicago she thought crime and poverty
and stranger danger. She had won $500 in a bingo game at St. Pius
and spent it on two beautiful maxi dresses, one a gauzy cotton
in light green, the other ticked in blue and white, and platform
sandals for height. The music that month was all Philadelphia
Freedom and He Don't Love You. My two best friends
and I met the bus in the parking lot of a strip mall on First Avenue.
My mother made me a Swiss cheese and peanut butter sandwich
though we also got a $2 voucher for McDonald's along the way
We stayed at the Palmer House, boys on one floor and girls
two floors below. We went to the Ivanhoe Dinner Theater,
to the Shedd Aquarium, to the Adler Planetarium, to Grant Park,
to Lincoln Park Zoo, to Old Town and New Town.

The best part for me: Chicago kids in Lincoln Park
yelling *are you from Iowa, you must be from Iowa,*
your pants are too short! to the despair
of my wannabe fashionable classmates.

On the way back the chaperones asked for a vote:
Who would rather live here than Cedar Rapids?
No one but one or two of us. The thing
is, at that very moment they asked we were riding past
my future, literally my current home high (23 stories)
on LSD (Lake Shore Drive) I not even noticing
its unprepossessing cinder block façade—like some kind
of metaphor—blowing past my years-to-be in St. Louis,
Champaign, Naperville, the marriage that took my 20s,
getting closer, closer to the shelter of a roofless sky,
an endless horizon where at dawn I cross the Drive
with my ninth grade self to catch butterflies on our tongue
as every cat and boy we've let rub up against us between then
and now follows, but that part never shows up in pictures,
and we never write this down.

Certaines choses ne changent jamais.

The Lake, big and old as the universe will laugh and love
us forever and ever, outliving us all: the Ivanhoe
long turned into a Binnie's Beverage Depot,
New Town reverted to mere East Lakeview,
the Palmer House in receivership, my parent's VW
sold for scrap, mother gone since 1986,
father since 2004, amen.

ON THE CUSP OF THE POSE

Because it was the 70s, and I was a teenager,
I used to hang my low cut button fly jeans
on the clothesline, exposed to the sun
and rain to get the perfect fade;

wore them with a white knit peasant top
which my friend's friend's boyfriend
once soiled with distinct handprints that my mother
laughed about because it was the 70s, and I

was a teenager. My ears remain/ed unpierced virgins.
I wore a blush on a thick stick that changed color on my face,
bought from a florescent store that smelled of industrial peonies,
hairspray, and compressed air, and sounded like instrumental
versions of 60s hits.

Never binge-vomited any alcohol nor food;
kept it, keep it, all inside, instead. My mom's friend
insisted all teenagers in the 70s were on drugs
but I wasn't then and not now: no statins, bone
boosters or hormones,

though my hair keeps getting lighter. I had a series of boyfriends
with red cars and my compulsion to repeat defeat: replete.
So while times have changed, I haven't really; no more than
a tree does, adding rings and frosting leaves,
still a budding column of sap
rooted and reaching.

Three Dates With Harry Chapin: Story Songs

December 14, 1977 Civic Center, Cedar Rapids Iowa:
I Wanna Learn a Love Song

I wore a chambray denim shirt with black velveteen collar and cuffs. L and I held hands in the cheap seats *"You can always count on the cheap seats!"* We were seniors in high school, in love, although we never said so, and he was into Harry.

That spring L started playing soccer and quit calling me. Eventually he married one of our high school classmates, had two daughters, re-embraced religion and became a paperback writer.

June 28, 1979 Southern Illinois University Edwardsville Outdoors:
A Better Place to Be

It was my idea. I wore denim cut-offs and a gauzy white top. Hot and humid, and eventually a thunderstorm raged over. My college boyfriend B waited with me in line in the downpour for Harry to kiss me.

Ended badly, when a few months later, I would meet the man I would marry.

April 24, 1980 Kiel Opera House St. Louis:
Dreams Go By

My 20th birthday. I made the plans and bought the tickets. I started crying mid-concert, because Harry was singing all the songs in the wrong order, and I felt responsible. I cried all over R's short sleeve button-down shirt, and he said he was honored. Just over a year later we eloped.

A few months after that Harry died. I kept the mustard yellow T-shirt with the line drawing of a guitar for a long time.

We got divorced, but I still feel like a widow.

Show Tunes

Ex texting
quotations, marked:
"I know all about your
standards…" Because July:
    Music Man.
last month was June's
    Carousel
bustin' out
all over.
(If I loved…)

Next month:
    State Fair
(Iowa, again, home state).

"…Irish imagination…" I know
he is drinking red
"…Iowa stubbornness…"
wine
"…library full of
books…" for his heart.
September, December
    Fantasticks.

May, always
    Camelot

Last line, un-
punctuated:
Don't you ever
think about being
…?
almost like being: it's always

Brigadoon   Groundhog Day.

WORK FRIENDS

I wanted to be in the cafe with you by now,
or better still in your backyard swimming pool

sitting on the white ceramic steps, leaning my back
against the arm rail, water against my legs,

the sun toasting my arms, one hefting a Perrier,
the other a mojito, listening to you laugh,

but it's my first day back to work and everyone wants
something. Meetings beget sidebars, beget private convos

and investigatory investigations and I keep reaching for my phone,
but can't even text you because my interruptions

are having interruptions and I worry you've not texted
me, sitting in the parking lot on your birthday,

no less, and not long after some minor surgery,
waiting, presumably, but who knows; maybe you passed

out, your hair crumpled against the driver's side window,
or left for some childcare emergency, streaking black rubber.

Worse, I need your help on some of this stuff,
but we are trying to model worklife balance for one another,

while at the same time I am also trying to perform
the necessary role of committed professional—

there's satisfaction in it and self-importance, too—
helping people feel like they are relaxing at a cafe

or in a pool themselves, versus always rushing
them to get to the point already so I can decompress,

like I was supposed to on vacation,
and, perhaps, did too well or not quite enough,

what with, every night, sleeping with Billy Collins,
meaning his books, under my pillow.

Mistaken Identity

I thought I saw you at Piazza Navona
in my stupor of prosecco and limoncello,
jet lag and Euro-urban travel-hiking. Easter egg
lady: pink-faced, yellow hair, blue eyes; you're
a type, for sure; neither common nor un, and may-
be I am, as well, if not the same, though we both
like the similar things; it's uncanny we've not run
into each other before, closer to home.
I always have an eye out for you, I often wish
I could call you up as in the days before texting
or even email, let alone social media,
and have you help me make sense
of some crazy thing in my life. It's never

you though, and maybe never was:
wasn't you, it was me. I used to think
friends were easy to come by, replenished
and refreshed like groceries, the seasons,
same but different; variations on a theme;
accumulated like shoes, curated and plucked
from the closet as needed, exactly as I left
them. Now I know it's more like research,
or a poem, how one begets another down
the line, possibly skipping generations,
an evolution of sorts, that we prepare
ourselves each one for a later one in hopes
that we can be what someone else needs most
at some given, random time and place.

As Told To

Occupation: self-care and waste
management. No destiny to fulfill. Produce:
nothing but feces and fur. Work:
from home, naked.
Have a live-in with thumbs
who hunts, grooms, sleeps with me;
she keeps strange hours and has too many
interests, in my opinion, though she is
a volunteer, so her price is right.

Found her at that hostel where I bit
everyone else. Would have bit her, too,
but her hair-smell made drowsy my limbs,
like my mama's belly filling mine,
so instead I licked her ear:
savory, sweetbitter, sour, and salt.

For kicks, I look through glass at birds
and bugs—not at or in it, nor see my image
in her eyes, reflection not being my jam
but sure as I guard her bed:
face-forward, door-toward, building bones
and healing wounds with soothing roar,
we know we make each other's home,
me and the one with thumbs,
writing this down.

HOSPICE

I want to die
a morphine fiend,
like my M-browed
tabby, Mandy. I made
a tent of striped fur, shot

her up; read her love
poems; sang lullabies.
She danced and chirped
her gratitude. No

Chemo—
(o, Mother!)
therapy.

Now I glimpse her
in every successive
cat, (as, I admit, my Major
Boyfriends sometimes blur
together in my synapses)

hoping you, love,
will likewise, not soon
but often, remember me.

OVERTIME

They no longer give kittens
away to the likes of me
and social media
generally approves.

It's one kind of pang to outlive
your animal companions,
but to think you won't
is next level.

Lord willing, those green bananas
will ripen in time, but they are only
.62 per pound.

All those trips I assumed were prefatory,
preparatory introductions?
(Always leave something unseen to go back
to! like Delphi!) Most were last chances.
Was it, is it, better to know or not?

Rare times I said to self: self, I will never,
ever do that ever again! Thank god!
Other times, abortive attempts,
realizing it's over, not even
remembering
the last time:

    Wear a bikini.
    Go on a first date.
    Work in an office.
    Job interview (?)

Pantyhose: the mass rebellion. My legs
itch remembering those plastic eggs
in the spinning rack at the drugstore,
early adopter of their cancellation.

May I never say: had I known I was going to live
this long I would have stolen that kitten.

PROFESSIN'

When I grow up I want to be a department chair,
said pretty much no one ever.

Nor any middle management job but especially that:
those who can't profess, mother other professors.

But *every woman wants to be a mother*, said the tall, Nordic man
after I mentioned that while I worked, back then, in a hospital,
I'd never stayed in one as an inpatient.

But you said you'd been   married,
is what he'd said right before
and I'd stared at him, confused, thinking he thought every wife
(or at least every divorcee) had not just eyes blackened
and arms broken but internal bleeding, concussions, hematomas,
when he only meant labor, delivery, and recovery.

But maybe I wanted but couldn't,
or I got my baby
not at the hospital
but from China or Russia, or Mawali
although I never did. (Have or want.)
Not to mention (though I am just about to)
the remoter possibility of home
(or cab or ambulance) birth.
And what did being married
have to do with it?
(I ask, rhetorically.)

Because nowadays we all agree it is fine
to be a single mother and/or for that matter lesbian, trans, bi, etc.
(Those latter not considered choices, so much as identities.)
It's all good...so long as a woman is a mother
or wants or wanted to be.

I don't owe anyone an explanation.
But I never wanted children
or to be a department chair.

And yet, here I am: a department
chair with no children, explaining.

EXCLAMATIONS OF THE FEMININE GENDER

I have a facility correctional:
voice sentenced to be passive;
imperative I be interrogative?

Were I to be infinitively subjunctive
you would be conditional,
call out my irregular,
semi-archaic, italicized *mood*
punctuated with period.

I'd contract
become fragment
abandons subject-verb agreement
runs on committing disorderly speech
acts, inverted, do sense that make you know I mean
what sorry not a negative double.

THE LAST WAVE

I always had to watch my husband swim. More than just watching, I tried to become him as he swam, parallel to the beach, his pale limbs sweeping through the blue ocean's froth-dotted waves. I knew that if I focused hard enough he'd swim on back to me and everything would be all right, I could at least summon a lifeguard before it was too late. It was meditation or the opposite; he was my lotus or anti-lotus. I can't remember the moment I faltered; no doubt there were many such, but one was definitive, or perhaps merely cumulative, the last wave.

THREE CURSES

I.

My mother was 17, orphaned by cancer,
about to be married when she saw the blood.
She thought she was injured or dying
of the family curse.

II.

They used to say cramps were all in our heads
And true, when fifth grader I sat in the school
nurse's office, or lay on the cot, away
from the stress of the classroom,

I felt better.

But how to explain the agony at twenty?
I could not have in any way wished
that upon my aspirationally pristine self:
newly married, sweating, incontinent, trembling.
Or ten years later, shakily presenting in suits to suits.

Later they said the worst pain is childbirth,
and the worst cramps are as bad as labor.

For sixty days a year times forty years
I patched together regimes of Advil, alcohol, exercise,
sugar, sex, eventually hormones, and, unlike many,
now, so scared that the train pulling up to the station
will jump its tracks, I was and remain ecstatic
at this journey's termination.

III.

Write the woman's name on a piece of paper. It won't hurt her,
they assured me. It only keeps her from further hurting you.

Put it in a plastic container, sealed in your freezer.
Something happened.

    Something terrible.

I hope she learned from it.

    I hope I did.

Paying it Forward

Almost every month I worried until it came
I was intact, virginal, but PMS rendered me paranoid
visions of sperm seeping as advice columnists

of the era insisted they could, through the pants
of a boy, the dress of a girl, while dancing upright,
even likelier in barer, more horizontal encounters,

penetration unnecessary, ejaculation optional.
I got married; eschewed hormones. Slips occurred
yet I could not imagine motherhood.

After the divorce I took the pills for five varicose
years, bubbling with nausea with each daily dose,
my orgasms muffled and far away,

my fake periods viscous as pudding.
When I stopped and the inevitable occurred, yes,
it was my own grown human fault.

At the clinic a few blocks from my house,
already bleeding as if in anticipation; a woman
was retching, a girl was crying. They gave me a test

to confirm then told me it was chemical,
no procedure needed. I handed them all my sweaty
cash for those less lucky, more deserving, than I.

HARSH MENTORING

They say by sixty, one begins to leave
the earth. For me, the year of no sleeping
was followed by the year of no eating.
It's amazing what one can do without!

I'd always tended toward (skewed) diffuse,
meaning to dissolve, disperse, evanesce—
not so much to frolic in the prolix.

Very confused by how everything
works now, or doesn't, all that self-service,
so there's no one to blame but the victim:
so-called efficiency takes forever.

I know I'm irreplaceable, but you?
Don't worry. You won't exactly be worse,
merely as bad in a different way.

DIFFERENT FOLKS

When bullying first became a thing
talked about, a high school classmate
said to me well, we don't have to worry
about you   killing
yourself: you're too chicken.

She was not not right: as a child
I used to run away from home
as far as the tree in the front of our yard,
(although to be fair, our house
was set far from the street).

They say a third of us hang back from danger
like wary canaries who sense, yet don't succumb,
taking protective measures, free-riders, social
loafers; letting the rest rush in, dauntless,

not doing our fair share, and true:
I'd be a terrible firefighter or soldier,
and if I'd been Assigned Male at Birth,
there'd have been worse hell to pay.

But I did get away, first to college
and then the city and like they say
it got a lot better, but some things
remain the same: that bully's

now a lawyer, manically signaling virtue.
Since then, a thousand times, everywhere,

I go, I run into her   clones,
although: *no one knows exactly*
                 what makes anyone else

     the way they are,
my self reminds myself, the teacher
who writes   sad poems.

Motion Sickness

I always have a trip pending, to stave off death.
Sometimes I stack plans up, three or four ahead
of time as insurance against lesser disaster.

Before I go, I experience bouts of vertigo.
How can I fit one more disruption
into the dizzy mosaic of my life?

Once I'm strapped in like an astronaut,
I'm forced to loosen up inside, over time.
Like an embryo, I grow in every direction,

then pop out, squalling and full of awe:
everything extra loud and bright,
I dream, awake, asleep, my past life

periodically forgotten; become confused
about which time and place is realer than the other.
I learn to walk and talk, fit in, find my path, mature.

I love when it rains on my last day
away, like an omen, calling me home.
When I get back, I feel like I flew a plane,

planned a city, built a museum, wrote a library,
ruled a queendom and liberated the populace.

Let Me Be Frank

(O'Hara, that is), just for this poem, but as a woman,
though our noses, mine and Frank's, are unfortunately similar,
and not to flatter myself, as I don't hang around with painters,
but management consultants and professors, but let's you be my
Vincent Warren, my adorably lithe dancer-lover, (but straight, and
the dancer part being metaphorical in your case) and I told
you all this before but it bears repeating: you are smart,
and all, with both abstractions and mechanics, can solve logic
problems and fix sinks and such, whereas I am messy and break
things and am imaginative and empathic,
but you are at least as well-traveled and sophisticated
as I, and we both like art
equally well, but had you not explained *Las Meninas*
to me I never would have finished my MFA,
and we both like to eat more than to cook
so we go out to Remington's or Eddie V's or Joe's Stone Crab,
or one of the Rosebuds or Osterias
and you always pay and encourage me to order prime rib
or Dover sole, and share a Caesar or burrata & beet salad and lava
cake dessert with you, but to drink we only ever order tap water,
never wine, spirits, or even soft drinks, (no Coke, no Pepsi)
and I used to get miffed when you'd crow
about our frugality, peering at the tabs of other patrons
as you plop extra helpings of lobster ravioli on my plate,
and bag up leftovers for me to eat the next day,
when all you eat at home (like Vincent) is yogurt,
so I mean I'm cool with tap water, despite the occasional server
disdain, and even though I enjoy craft cocktails or sipping splits
of prosecco with the girls and have been known to frequent
the liquor aisle at Trader Joe's, and brew iced tea by the gallon,
it's not that I felt deprived so much as bargain basement—
you like to call yourself "price-sensitive," *did that extend to me?* —and I
also wondered whether you'd toasted some past

(or, god forbid, would toast some future) fling with Top Shelf
because she was "worth it," but I pretty much got over it, because
the food and, most of all the company and the conversation
your laughter, your dimples, your eyelashes, are *worth* it.

I mean to say: if John Ashbery's contemporary and heterosexual
equivalent offered to sweep me off somewhere exotic
and all-inclusive of beverage, I'd tell him I'd rather, to be Frank,
drink tap water with you.

Telling

You tell me I left a gold-beige stain:
concealer marring white hotel towel.
You, for whom everything's a text,
subject to rigorous interpretation,
tell me how we treat a towel is fractal
of our footprint on the world at large.

Do you remember those Turkish carpets,
near the Virgin Mary house?—each with flaw;
small, deliberate; highlighting our humble role
as servants of some Higher Power,
and if you tell me my error renders
our union besmirched as a stained towel,

I'll tell you I am double-bound: the need
to hide my imperfection ensures its revelation.

CONFESSION (WITH REDACTIONS)

S said I should just go ahead and [verb] [Proper Noun] already
since 'as far as we knew' *you* were [verb-ing] everyone you met.

But I never believed that!

And besides I never wanted to [verb] [Proper Noun], I only
wanted to [(different) verb] him.

III

SOMETHING ELSE

"Don't be too timid and squeamish about your actions. All life is an experiment." —Ralph Waldo Emerson

Two Half Sonnets

I.

Would you compare me to a bowl of pho?
My blood test says that I'm more like *foie gras*.
Physicians seem to think that's something bad!
My cat sure seems to find me delicious
as the salt lick at the edge of a pond.

I can't stop sonneting—is that a thing?
It will make work emails interesting.

II.

My butt's been the bait of many switches,
as I'm more of an emotional wench,
squandering my feelings on the unworthy.

Remaining imperfectly iambic,
not to say clueless of prosody,
I have all the requisite credentials;
may as well repurpose as poetry.

PSYCHE GOES TO THE FARMER'S MARKET

When your jealous sisters
goad you into spilling hot wax
on your sleeping husband's
heaving pecs, to see if he's a secret monster
(back story: you were the weirdo beauty queen
who couldn't get a prom date
and finally bagged your prince)
when clearly you're the psycho,
so he leaves and your mother-in-law
who never liked you sends you off on a series
of impossible tasks to earn back her son:
seeds, fleece, samples and   hell
as other people   plus some mystery ointment
there's no place
like the dreaded   Farmer's Market
for 1) stalls of seeds pre-sorted   sprouted
into green leaves you can trust
2) sheepish shoppers ramming before mid-day
naps   extruding DNA
3) that little bag that holds so much less than you need to
purchase   eagling your eye
and 4) so many people for you NOT to help   this
time   despite their pleas:
housing-challenged fellow citizens, kids pushing soccer-chocolate,
the lady who always needs just five dollars to get her train
back to Indiana.
Sunblocked, goggled, agog, overstimulated, jostled, cat-called:
the cost is clear, the benefits dubious, but done, done, done and
done; evidence bought and bagged with wearying, exhilarating
transactions.

Is discipline a muscle, developing, or well depleted?

Because that bogus, bonus jar you are supposed
to bring back to her   unopened:

whatever it is   have you not   earned it?

Don't you   deserve it?

Becoming Punxsutawney Phil (A Groudhog Day Film Ekphrasis)

White clouds, snow, blue sky and filter;
groundhog images replicating like the rodents
they represent; hands: ideas
of transformation in things.

How would you spend
eternity? Comic.
Let's live here;
(rent to start).

What if nothing we did mattered? Picaresque,
and refuted. See Phil C go from eating to feeding;
mocking to copying to emulation; smoking to CPR; that snow-
man turned ice sculpture; that mandala of groundhogs
near the end, ringing his head.

What if there were no tomorrow?
Tragic, but even planets and stars
die. Perhaps he was dead
from that first shower, a slip:
perhaps we all are dead,
but to die before the battle,
to murder our eager egos
as many times as needed,
is to have a brand new day
with nothing left to lose.

DEAR CAPITALISM,

I told my colleague
that, in the world,
he and I are the 1%;

he said, oh I guess
that may be what the world
thinks, and I said no

it's a true fact
I mean to say: math.
He and I reject

that reductive paradigm
but gravity
is what it is, believe

it or not. This is not a protest poem
nor love letter or break
up text. I can't quit

you, so why pretend
this is not/I am not/we
are not codependent?
The bots will overwrite

us, but in the mean
time we will optimize

worship workshop warship
as we outsource
poet-industrial complex-
ity and co-exist
like true crime
with true romance.

ADVICE ON THREE CONTEMPORARY CONUNDRUMS

I. *Adjustment Disorder*

How is being well-adjusted not just settling at best
And lacking empathy at worst
Like those people who suddenly think
They live in a simulated universe
Having just now noticed wrongness
Because it finally arrived *chez eux*
Though I guess it's a start

Calibrate your mal/adjustment
Just so

II. *Imposter Syndrome*

Their hair shakes over their faces like rain
Eyes covered they confess to all who listen
They secretly think they don't belong
And are maybe just fooling everyone

But it's not a secret because you literally told everyone
And everyone agrees they feel exactly the same
So you actually fit right in
And no one is fooling anyone

See *Adjustment Disorder*

III. *Toxic Masculinity*

Some fellow academics said that to use this term
Even in quotes was tantamount to a hate crime
Against men but who said anything about men
And too much anything is toxic even air water and sleep
So they asked if there was toxic femininity
So clever these academic fellows

It's actually the same thing
As every extreme alchemically transforms into its opposite
Enantiodromia

Not that anyone said anything about women
But speaking of women
Please see *Imposter Syndrome* for additional insight
Also *Adjustment Disorder*

You're welcome.

In the Thirst Economy

Poems are undervalued instruments;
perfect bargains for the right investor.
Not like those social media selfies:
this is what 50 looks like, attracting
horndogs and haters—at best, cheap thrills.
Trolling for compliments compliments trolls.

Some poets abhor the word submission.
But me, I call it topping from below.
If you despise my words, isn't that close,
closer to love than to indifference?
If you ignore them, you must just be blind.
If you love them, no interpretation

necessary. When I lose, it's a lot-
tery, but when I win, I earned it all.

Say

In your next life you could be an orchid
or dandelion. Who's to say who's better?
Fragile beauty or gold grit? Seriously:
it takes all kinds. Literally: everything

is designed to be what it is, to do
as it does. You can stamp your tattoo
brand on the strategic plan like tramp
or angel, whatever your angle: hip or ankle.

Not to say it doesn't matter, but let's say
it doesn't: matter, like energy's neither born
nor aborted. There's a non-coercion clause,
only death and taxes inevitable. I'm not here

to advocate the path of least resistance; I'm only
the observer whose very observation changes
the observed, as if such absurdity were even possible:
white cloud over thistle, ghost rising from swamp.

YOUR PERFECT POEM

I don't normally leave a comment,
but I must insist on this exception:
your delicious poem was a hit
with my crew! I only made
a few small tweaks:

ingredient-wise, we like it a little less bland,
so I spiced it up with some adjectives
and I switched out the moth
conceit with a butterfly (monarch,
the only kind I buy) for a pop of color.

We are not that into peasant cuisine,
so I made a reduction of the hills and trees
motif and swapped it with a cityscape.

And for an entrée, it was a bit delicate
for hearty appetites, so added some stanzas
for volume.

Didn't have time to bake it as long
as you, given my demanding day job,
family responsibilities, and volunteer
work. But we think it came out even better;
at least more to our taste.

Anyhoo, these blog poems are usually mediocre, but yours?
Sheer perfection! Could not be happier with this recipe.
Yum! I'll be sharing.

Resolution

C.G Jung's last words were to his nurse,
who some say was his mistress,
and lived with him and his wife:
let's have a very nice red wine tonight.

I think a lot about endings:
this, too, shall pass;
all good things must end;
all's well that ends well;
it all ends up OK in the end;
if it's not OK, it's not the end;
fire or ice, bang or whimper.

Studies on medical procedures
say not to end on a pain point,
but something pleasant that soothes
the patient and eases the transition
from painworld to the ordinary
one of intermittent dread and relief,
so the lasting impression is the latter.

Jung's contemporary, Matisse,
the painter, lost his abdominal muscles
and ability to steady a paintbrush
after cancer surgery, but he still saw the world
in paintings, as sculpture, and cut shapes and colors
with scissors, applied with long sticks; still the same man,
partly blind for a time,
earlier in his life
from peering at colors
with too much intensity:
a pause to clear the palette.

SELF-PORTRAIT AS POET

Poet, you mama's girl, so bad at volleyball, first dates, job
interviews, other crucial life skills, your albatross of asymmetry
flung floorward like an eloquent glove, ironic as that yellow
yield sign on Chicago Avenue, permanently pavement-flattened.
Poet, so many hard things they said you couldn't do that you did
(make a lot of money, live alone in the city); usual things assumed
you would when you wouldn't (drive and have babies).
Didn't want to get married, but married you got, and the divorce?
Also his idea.

Poet, there's no ADA accommodation for it: every job
you get too many promotions, then get fired for creative excess
(*how is that even a thing?*) All devotion, no discipline. Your right
to take up space in a shrinking universe, a dying planet:
dubious and openly debated.

Poet, you manqué, *jolie-laide, savant*-lite, immature, elderly
oxymoron, you want to be blameless, but that ship
has left its bottle; the genie: genuine, generative,
generous, curious, has granted her curse
  to elude mediocrity at every cost.

But

Poet, every potion has its antidotes we are doomed to forget:
the brain is redundancy-replete, evolved toward integration, gaps
filling as we speak: neurons wiring firing fusing; time's arrow
is unidirectional, but only in the material world, and even
there, while sensitive dependence on initial conditions

sets a trajectory, and airplanes off course, mostly they land
as planned, (almost) always. Poet, that genie was you
all along. Not dead yet is your best feature.

Something Else

Her muse caresses her awake, urging to abandon her formal plan, her notes, her slides. She feels the sweet trembling in her limbs, pictures her performance as a flowing river, defining the landscape.

Arrives, beams at the moderator, steps on the stage. Glances down to see her bare leg sticking out from her short pink chenille robe, ends in slightly hairy-chested toes.

Curious.

Draws a breath, weak and shaky, powering through.

The stage does not consume her.

She becomes a curiosity, large as the auditorium, larger, Curiosity Itself, infinite, a floating cloud.

Not as she had hoped, before or later, or ever; something else entirely. But, nonetheless, something.

Acknowledgements

I would like to thank all my teachers, notably Major Jackson, Nan Cohen, Brenda Hillman, Martha Silano, Beth Ann Fennelly, Peter Campion, Jared Joseph, and Gail Mazur; my loyal readers, notably Jane Grady and Josie Corbett; and the editors who chose my poems for their prior publication, notably C. M. Tollefson, Sandra Fluck, and Kim Chinquee.

And thank you, Saddle Road Press, for making this book a reality.

And, most of all, thank you Beau, my first, last, and (almost) always reader!

The following poems were published previously, some in slightly different versions:

Another Chicago Magazine: "In the Thirst Economy," "Since You've Been Gone," "The Words"

Beyond Words: "GirlWor(l)d"

Black Fox Literary Magazine: "Corpse Pose"

Cathexis Northwest Press: "After Nemerov," "Aubade," "The Color of my Eyes," "On the Cusp of the Pose," "Psyche Goes to the Farmer's Market," "Resolution," "Spare," "Those Who Don't Believe in Ghosts," "Wavicle" (as "Wave")

Cleaver: "Show Tunes"

Closed Eye Open: "Confession (With Redactions)," "Mistaken Identity"

Dillydoun Review: "Overtime," "The Poem Everyone Writes," "Remembering the Sabbath"

Faux Moir:" "Birds of the Midwest," "Trippin'"

Griffel: "Before We Met"

HASH: "The Last Wave," "Lookers," "Something Else"

JMWW: "Standard Time"

Lighthouse Weekly: "Three Curses," "Paying it Forward"

Maudlin House: "Advice on Three Contemporary Conundrums"

New World Writing: "As Told To," "How to be It," "Say," "Three Dates with Harry Chapin," "Your Perfect Poem"

Nine Cloud Journal, "Becoming Punxsutawney Phil: A Groundhog Day Film Ekphrasis"

Prometheus Dreaming: "Hospice," "The Infinite Comings of Age"

Quartz, "Trajectory" (as "Sensitive Dependence on Initial Conditions")

Sad Girls Club: "Exclamations of the Feminine Gender"

The Scapegoat Review: "The Constancy of Forgetting" (as "On the Constancy of Forgetting")

Sky Island Journal: "Carapace"

Wild Roof Review: "Walk"

The Write Launch: "About Last Night," "Chicago (After Ginsberg)" "Dear Capitalism," "Different Folks," "Landlocked Lament," "Linn Junction," "On the Way to Conception," "Plus Ça Change," "Professin'," "Self Portrait as Poet," "The Spring-Bringer," "Telling," "wake up," "When You Spot Your Flower," "Work Friends"

Some of these poems were previously included in my chapbook *About Time,* published in 2022 by Cathexis Northwest Press.

About Julie Benesh

Julie Benesh grew up in Iowa, has lived in Chicago for more than 30 years and is the recipient of an Illinois Arts Council Grant. She is author of the poetry chapbook *About Time* and has published stories, poems, and creative nonfiction in *Tin House*, (including *Bestial Noise, A Tin House Fiction Reader*), *Crab Orchard Review, Florida Review, JMWW, Maudlin House, Cleaver* and many other places.

She is a graduate of the MFA Program for Writers at Warren Wilson College, holds a PhD in human and organizational systems, and majored in English at Washington University in St. Louis. She worked in the organization development field for many years and is currently a full professor and department chair of organizational leadership and business psychology.

She frequently presents at conferences on the synergies among workplace outcomes and workforce expressive writing. She teaches writing craft workshops at the Newberry Library and is currently polishing her debut, long-anticipated short story manuscript, *Flyover Girls*. *Initial Conditions* is her first published full-length book.

Printed in the USA
CPSIA information can be obtained
at www.ICGtesting.com
LVHW020538290224
773081LV00007B/164

9 798987 954140